MW00395775

© Copyright Academy of Surfing Instructors Pty Ltd

Published by the Academy of Surfing Instructors Pty Ltd
Bondi, New South Wales, 2026 Australia
www.academyofsurfing.com

Reprinted: July 2007
First published: September 2003

Cover photo credit: Alex Turoy

National Library of Australia
Cataloguing-in-Publication data:

ISBN 0-9751523-0-0
Learn to Surf for Beginners

Surfing is a dangerous sport. All care has been taken to give the best possible information in
this instruction manual. No responsibility is accepted for any illnesses or injuries incurred by
an individual when following the directions contained in this instruction manual. Any injuries
resulting from surfing are the sole responsibility of the individual who wilfully and knowingly
engages in a sport known to be dangerous.

KEEP ON SURFING

Masayuki Sato Photograph
www.mandn.com.

Foreword

by Nigel Hutton-Potts

This manual is the first in a series of Learn to Surf training resources produced by the Academy of Surfing Instructors (ASI). It aims to assist people to gain the necessary skills and knowledge required to surf with competence at the beginner level.

This instruction manual has been designed specifically with the beginner surfer in mind. It is, therefore, very simple and easy to read and understand. All areas have been covered to enable you to get up and riding in beginner surf conditions. It also includes special pointers on awareness and safety in the surf.

Use this manual as a basic guide to any potential barriers you come across as a new surfer.

There is no other book available that has the valued information contained in these pages to help you fast-track the development of your surfing skills.

ASI has established four levels for surfing skill and knowledge: beginner, intermediate, advanced and elite advanced. Once you have mastered the beginner level, you can then progress on to the more advanced levels.

The surfing world awaits you. Enjoy your surfing life.

Nigel has been surfing for over 30 years and is experienced in all aspects of surfing. He grew up in Bondi Beach, Australia and has devoted his life to surfing surf breaks around the world.

Nigel provides the "inside" on what surfing is all about and a wealth of tips and techniques, gained over the years, on the "how" to surf at all levels.

Academy of Surfing Instructors (ASI)

Academy of Surfing Instructors (ASI) specialises in education and accreditation for the recreational surfing industry. We develop and publish learn to surf books, DVDs, surfing lesson plans and curriculum. We train accredited surfing instructors and issue accreditation status to surf schools according to the ASI worldwide standard.

ASI Learn to Surf Training Resources

ASI publishes learn to surf manuals, DVDs, student workbooks, surfing lesson plans and curriculum from beginner to elite advanced surf skills. Learning to surf is now easier than ever.

ASI Accredited Surf Schools

ASI accredited surf schools are known for their high standards in surfing lesson delivery, equipment, service and safety. Each year, ASI accredited surf schools, undergo an extensive audit in all areas of their operations, staff and training because we want to make sure our standards are the best in the world.

ASI Accredited Surfing Instructors

Accredited Surfing Instructors are in demand! ASI surfing instructors and coaches are all trained to the highest standard in the world. Level 1 to Level 4. Former world champion, Cheyne Horan, is one of ASI's Master Surfing Coaches - be trained by the best.

Surfing books & DVDs / Website surfing directory

Check out the ASI website for an extensive range of DVDs and surf books. Purchase on-line. The Surfing directory lists a range of surfing related products and services. Find it at ASI.

Setting the world standard in surfing education
Contact us on +61 2 9365 4170 (In Australia – Ph: 02 9365 4170)
email: info@academyofsurfing.com
www.academyofsurfing.com

Contents

Contents (continued)

Contents *(continued)*

Contents *(continued)*

Introduction
Welcome to a new life...

Welcome to the start of your new life as a surfer. Surfing is more than a sport, it's a lifestyle. Free, natural and exhilarating. It is about having fun and learning exciting new skills.

There is nothing quite like the experience of catching one of nature's forces – the breaking wave. You are able to harness that power to speed you along the wave and perform a variety of manoeuvres.

Every wave you ride will be unique. Each wave has its own challenges to test your skills.

In order to surf, you need to know the skills of surfing and you also need to know about the surf environment, surf safety and your equipment. Greater knowledge in these areas is the only way to improve your surfing.

This Beginner's instruction manual covers all these areas so that you will have a strong base on which to develop your surfing skills.

So enjoy this lifestyle away from the stress of everyday life. Have fun, live life and go off!

Chapter 1

Surfing Background

> **Outcomes...**
> At the end of this chapter, you will be able to:
> - Understand where surfing originated
> - Identify some surfing spots around the world
> - Explain the difference between professional and amateur surf competitions
> - Explain what surf culture is

1 - History

Surfing is generally acknowledged to have originated in the Hawaiian and Polynesian Islands around two hundred years ago. Early European explorers observed people paddling out in the water on wooden planks then catching a wave, standing up and riding it back to the shore.

Since these early sightings, surfing has come a long way to where we are now. In just about every country in the world, that has a coast with waves, people are taking up this fun sport.

2 - Terminology

When you start surfing, you will find that it has words and expressions that are unfamiliar. Most sports have their own vocabulary and jargon. With surfing, you need to learn a new language if you want to be regarded as truly dedicated.

Surf language is an evolving language. New terminology develops as new products and surf manoeuvres are discovered and may even be particular to different countries or local regions.

We use surf terms throughout this manual. There is a short list of these at the back of this manual. You will become familiar with these terms as you use them more frequently and as you develop your surfing expertise.

3 - Surf Spots

There are many famous surfing spots around the world. They are famous for their perfect and/or consistent waves. Some of these include:

- **Waimea Bay** - Hawaii (famous for big waves)
- **Pipeline** - Hawaii (the world's most famous tube, reef break)
- **Jefferies Bay** - South Africa (famous for its long right hand point break)
- **Grajagan Bay** - (G-Land), Java, Indonesia (famous for its big left hand point/reef break)
- **Uluwatu** - Bali, Indonesia (famous for its reef break)
- **Margaret River** – Western Australia (famous for its river mouth break)
- **Kirra** – Queensland, Australia (famous for its fast right hand tube).

Waimea Bay, Hawaii

Margaret River, Australia

Uluwatu, Bali

4 - Surf Events

Dedicated surfing professionals compete regularly for the title of world champion surfer each year. These events are held at famous surf spots around the world. These events attract major sponsors such as Xcel, Quiksilver, Billabong, Ripcurl, Rusty, to name a few.

Surf competitions are also held for amateur surfers from juniors (grommets) right through to mature aged senior surfers. If you are interested in competitions, ask at your local surf shop or surf school for surf events happening in your area.

5 - Surf Culture

Surf culture is outdoor, healthy and active. Being able to enjoy the simple things in this life such as good friends, having fun and respecting nature, are at the heart of surf culture.

The surfer's life centres around the beach and where the waves are. When the surf is up, surfers are out there chasing the waves. Then when the waves die down, it's back to regrouping with friends, exchanging surf stories, and waiting for the next swell.

Chapter 2
The Surfing Environment

Outcomes...

At the end of this chapter, you will be able to:

- Explain how waves are formed
- Identify the type of wave suitable for surfing
- Identify the parts of the wave
- Measure wave height
- Look after our surfing environment

1 - Waves

Waves are the most important part of surfing. Without waves, you cannot surf.

Large storms out to sea generate most waves when strong winds blow across the water's surface. The wind causes friction on the water, causing it to form into swells (unbroken waves).

As this swell enters shallow water, water particles compress, forcing the swell to rise up until it reaches a point where the top throws over as a breaking wave.

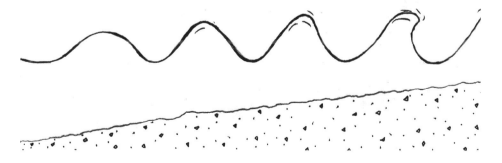

Waves often come in groups, commonly known as a "set". There are usually three to five waves in a set. Often the third wave in a set will be the largest.

1.1 Different Types of Waves

There are two different types of waves – the plunging (dumping) wave and the peeling wave.

1.1.1 Plunging or Dumping Wave

The plunging wave is also called a close-out or a dumper. The whole wave throws over, breaking all at once. These waves can be dangerous if you are caught under the breaking part of the wave.

Stay away from dumping waves – they are not suitable for surfing.

✗ Dumping Wave
Not suitable for surfing.

The whole wave face breaks at once.

1.1.2 Peeling Wave

The other type of wave is the peeling wave.

The peeling starts at one point of the wave and continues to break across the wave face as the wave comes into the shore.

These waves are the best for surfing.

✔ **Peeling Wave**
Suitable for surfing.

Gently breaking, peeling from one point along the face of the wave. Not too large for the beginner

1.2 Parts of the Wave

In order to surf, you should become familiar with the different parts of the wave. These are:

Wave face: the concave unbroken part of a wave where most manoeuvres can be performed.

Lip: the top or crest of the wave. It's the part that rises up, then throws out and over.

Wave curl: the peeling part of the wave as it breaks.

Trough: the bottom of the wave.

Foam or soup: the broken part of the wave. It's also called the white-water.

Impact zone: the place where all the force of the breaking wave hits the trough.

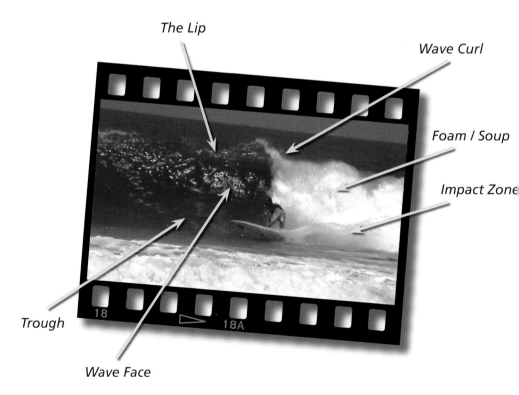

The Lip

Wave Curl

Foam / Soup

Impact Zone

Trough

Wave Face

1.3 Wave Height

It is also a good idea to know how wave height is measured so that you do not go into surf beyond your ability.

Wave height is generally measured from the lip to the trough.

Some surfers call wave heights by reference to your body e.g. knee high, waist high, head high and double over head, etc.

2 - Environmental Impact

Surfing, itself, has little impact on the natural environment. The surfboard is used in the water and so no damage is caused.

However, here are some ways that you can care for the surfing environment around you:

Place your rubbish in a bin or take it away with you, if there aren't any bins.

If you are not near a toilet, human waste should be disposed off appropriately (e.g. dig a hole).

Be careful not to dislodge rocks or other natural formations.

Do not disturb plants and animals including coral on reefs.

Be aware of trampling and breaking vegetation. Keep to marked tracks or routes wherever possible.

If you take any animals such as dogs, make sure they are tied up safely, as they could frighten or kill local wildlife.

Before lighting a campfire, check local fire regulations. Remove any traces of the campfire so the environment remains as it was. Instead of using wood from the local area, you could use a fuel stove.

Do not create noise that will disturb others.

Be aware of any cultural sites or customs so as not to cause offence to the local people.

Chapter 3

Personal Surfing Safety

Outcomes...

At the end of this chapter, you will be able to:

- Understand the importance of swimming skills
- Identify techniques for self rescue and self survival in the water
- Apply sun safety practices
- Identify the symptoms and treatment of heat exhaustion
- Identify the symptoms and treatment of hypothermia

1 - Swimming Skills

Having good swimming skills is a pre-requisite for surfing. You need to be able to swim because if your leg-rope or surfboard breaks, you could have a long swim back to shore.

You should have confidence to swim in the surf and be able to float and tread water.

2 - Self Rescue

If you get into trouble in the water, try to attract the attention of a lifeguard or any others who may be able to help you. Do not hesitate to call for help if you are unsure. It is better to get help early than wait until you are exhausted.

Use recognised signals to attract attention. In lifesaving, the signal for requiring assistance is waving one arm to and fro above your head.

Always remain with your surfboard, or any broken parts, for flotation. If you are without your surfboard and not able to get to the shore or safety, float and/or tread water until help arrives.

3 - Fitness

When you are surfing, you are constantly using your muscles – especially your arms, shoulders and legs. The more toned your muscles, the easier it will be to surf. When you are not surfing, you can do exercises at home to keep you in good surfing condition.

4 - Sun Safety

Surfers spend a lot of time in the sun and can easily get sunburn.

Exposure to the sun's ultraviolet rays is the major cause of sunburn. Sunlight is usually strongest between the hours of 11 am to 3 pm. The suns rays reflecting off the water can also increase the intensity.

To avoid sunburn:

- wear sunscreen on all exposed parts of your body. Re-apply regularly.

- wear protective clothing (e.g. rash vest)

- wear hat and sunglasses when watching the surf

- be especially careful between the hours of 11 am and 3 pm

5 - Dehydration

Make sure you drink enough fluids (non-alcoholic) before going surfing so you do not become dehydrated.

If you plan to go to the beach for a long time, take enough water with you.

6 - Heat Exhaustion and Heat Stroke

Heat exhaustion and heat stroke can occur when you are surfing in the hot sun and in hot climates.

When your body heats up, it may not cool itself effectively. Your body normally cools down as sweat evaporates. However, in humid climates, evaporation of sweat is slower due to the amount of moisture in the air.

Symptoms of **Heat Exhaustion** include:	Symptoms of **Heat Stroke** include:
✔ warm pink skin	✔ hot dry pale skin
✔ sweating	✔ not sweating
✔ vomiting	✔ sudden collapse
✔ cramps	✔ aggressiveness
✔ confusion	✔ restlessness
✔ headaches	✔ having a fit

If you have any of these symptoms, get into the shade or a cool place, cool yourself with water or fanning, drink water and seek medical aid, if necessary.

7 - Hypothermia

The opposite to heat stroke and heat exhaustion is hypothermia.

Hypothermia occurs when normal core body temperature of 37 degrees celsius or (98 degrees fahrenheit), drops below 35 degrees celsius (95 degrees fahrenheit).

As sea temperature is cooler than body temperature, anyone immersed in water without protection will lose body heat.

The amount of body heat you lose will depend on a number of factors:
- the time you are immersed in the water.
- the water temperature and wind.
- the amount of protective clothing or body fat.
- the level of activity.   The less activity, the quicker the loss of body heat.
- the effect of drugs such as alcohol which increases the loss of body heat.

If you start to feel cold, or start to shiver when surfing, make sure you get out of the water and get warm.

Seek out shelter from any wind.

Chapter 4

Surfing Hazards

> **Outcomes...**
> At the end of this chapter, you will be able to:
> - Identify rips and currents
> - Explain how to get out of a rip
> - Identify other surf hazards
> - Explain the "Golden Rule" of surfing safety

1 - Rips and Currents

Rips and currents are one of the major hazards surfers come across in the ocean. They are also the main cause of surf rescues.

A rip is a body of water that usually moves out to sea. When water comes into the shore, it has no-where else to go but back out to sea. The water forms a channel in one place and this is called a rip.

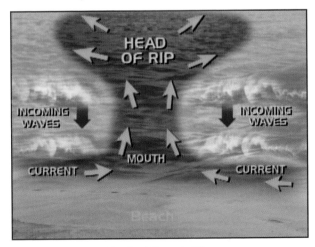

Typical Beach Rip

1.1 How to Identify Rips and Currents

You can identify rips by:

- A rippled appearance on the surface of the water, when the water around is generally calm.
- Discoloured water due to sand being stirred up from the ocean bottom.
- Foam, bubbles or debris on the surface of the water – moving out to sea.
- Waves breaking on both sides, but not in the middle, of a rip.

Examples of Rips

Rips can form between two sand banks causing a channel of smoother water as shown here. You can see the waves are breaking on either side of the channel.

To the beginner, this may seem a safe place to go into the surf because the water is smoother. But you could be carried out to sea further than you intended to go.

1.2 Getting out of Rips/Currents

Any person surfing or swimming in the ocean should be aware of rips and currents and their potential dangers. Rips can carry you out to sea. Some rips may only take you a little way out but others may take you out a long way.

Rips can require a lot of paddling and this can tire you out to the point of not being able to keep yourself afloat. A major problem is that if you get caught in a rip you may panic and try to paddle directly against it – furthering tiring yourself.

If you get caught in a rip, stay calm.

You can paddle across the rip in order to get out of it.

Do not paddle against, or into, the rip as you will tire yourself.

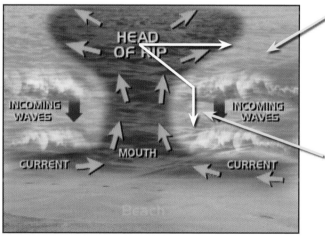

Poor or tired surfer to paddle / swim across the rip and then into shore.

Strong surfer can paddle / swim on an angle to the rip and then into the shore.

How to Escape From a Rip

Beware

- Stay very clear of rips until you learn to use them to your advantage.
- Always check the beach for rips before going into the water.
- On patrolled beaches check for posted signs identifying rips in the water. If you see these signs, stay well away from the rip.
- Ask the locals or surf lifeguards if you are unsure if any rips are present.

2 - Marine Creatures

Marine creatures generally do not get in a surfer's way however there are some creatures that surfers should be aware of.

- **Sharks** – come in all sizes. Often there can be small sharks swimming around reef areas that do not pose a threat to you. However, keep an eye out for larger ones. If you happen to see a shark, try to remain calm and head for the shore. Catch a wave in lying down.

- **Blue bottles / stingers** – have a translucent blue air sac and long blue tentacles that sting. The sting is extremely painful and can be dangerous if you are allergic to stings. If you are stung, remove the tentacle and apply an anti-stinging lotion. Look out for signs of them on the shore-line.

- **Sea snakes** – are highly venomous and if bitten, seek help immediately. They are generally found in tropical waters. If you see one, move away as quickly and carefully as possible. Use your surfboard to fend it off.

- **Jelly fish** – are generally harmless however some can be dangerous. It is best you avoid them.

- **Sea lice** - are usually found in tropical waters. You cannot see them in the water however you feel them by itching sensations that can become irritating. Try not to scratch as it only makes things worse.

- **Otters and seals** – are not dangerous but they may get in your way when surfing. So keep a look out at all times.

Marine creatures in the water may change depending on the location and season. So, always be on the look out and check with the locals or lifeguards before going into the water if you are unsure.

3 - Rocks

Be aware of any rocks in the area, including submerged/underwater rocks. At the beginner level, you should stay away from any rocks.

Potential signs of underwater rocks include swirling water on the surface and waves breaking when the water around is calm.

Usually the locals are well aware of dangerous rocks and avoid these areas. If unsure, ask the locals.

4 - Other people and watercraft

Always be aware of other people and other watercraft around you in the surf.

Before catching a wave, check that no-one is in your way and that there isn't another person already surfing along that wave towards you. If you don't check, you could hurt yourself or them or both of you.

You can avoid these situations by having a constant awareness of where you are in relation to all others.

Also, stay out of the way of more advanced surfers. They will soon get annoyed if you keep getting in their way.

5 - Own surfboard

Look out for your own surfboard. After a wipe-out, it can recoil quickly on its leg-rope and possibly hit you.

Come up with your hand first so you do not hit your head on your board should it be directly above or springing back at you.

6 - Waves

Large waves can be a hazard. They have a lot of power and can hold you under water and throw you around. Shore breaks are also a hazard if the waves are dumping.

Always keep your eyes out to sea. Never turn your back on the waves. They can suddenly form up and dump on you if you are not alert.

7 - Pollution

Be aware of any pollution in the water. There may be contaminated matter from spillages and storm-water ocean outlets which could make you ill.

At tropical locations, there may be coconuts or other floating debris to avoid. Some locations have a lot of seaweed.

If there is too much pollution in the water, it is best not to go surfing there.

The Golden Rule of Surfing Safety

Never go surfing in water that you are unsure of:-
where the surf is larger than your ability.

Ask yourself:
"would you still be able to swim in that surf and back to the shore if your leg-rope breaks and you lose your board?"

If you don't think so,
the best idea is not to go surfing until conditions are more suitable for you.

Chapter 5
Your Surfing Equipment

Outcomes...

At the end of this chapter, you will be able to:
- Identify 4 main surfboard shapes
- Identify the parts of the surfboard
- Attach a leg-rope
- Choose a surfboard for the beginner surfer
- Transport and carry your surfboard safely
- Apply wax to your surfboard
- Describe how to clean your surfboard
- Identify ways to store your surfboard safely
- Check your equipment for damage

1 - The Surfboard

Surfboards have changed dramatically over time as surfboard makers constantly strive to design better boards. The first surfboards were made from wood. Most surfboards today are made from light-weight foam and fibre-glass and other synthetic materials.

Surfboards come in all shapes and sizes. The board you choose to ride will depend on:

- style – a long board or short board
- the surf conditions
- the type of surf manoeuvres performed, and
- your height and weight

1.1 Surfboard Shapes

There are basically 4 types of surfboard shapes. These are:

Short Board
This board has a more pointed nose, is not as wide as the long board and the length is usually under 7 foot.
These boards are not very stable but are very manoeuvrable allowing you to do manoeuvres easily.

Gun
Is a short board shape but more tapered towards the nose and tail. The length is usually 7 to 9 foot or more. Guns are used for riding large waves. They still have some manoeuvrability but not as much as the short board.

The Fun Board
(also called a Mini-Mal)
The fun board is the same as the long board but with a length under 9 foot. These boards have a bit less stability but are more manoeuvrable than the long board.

The Long Board
(also called a Malibu)
The long board is a long, wide board with a rounded nose. Length is usually 9 foot and over. It is a stable board but not as manoeuvrable as the fun board.

1.2 Parts of the Surfboard

Even though the surfboard looks simple in design, each part is designed for a purpose.

Surfboard designers and shapers develop a reputation based on how well their surfboards perform in the waves. They usually have years of first hand experience of what makes a board perform well and a good understanding of the physics involved in surfing.

For all their shapes and sizes, surfboards have common parts.   These are:

Nose:	Front section of the surfboard
Deck:	Top of surfboard where you stand
Rails:	The sides (edge) of the surfboard between the deck and bottom
Bottom:	Underneath part of the surfboard
Tail:	Back section of surfboard
Plug:	Where the leg-rope is attached to the surfboard
Stringer:	The timber strip down the centre of fibre-glass surfboards providing strength
Fins:	Guiding rudders of the surfboard
Leg-rope:	Also called a leash is a specially designed cord that connects you and the surfboard.

Nose **Deck** **Leg-rope** **Plug**

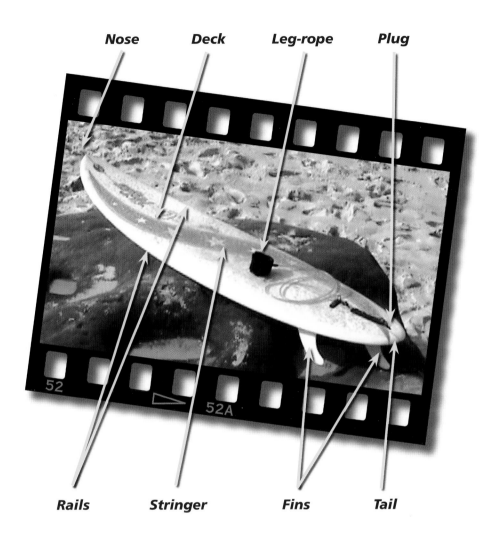

Rails **Stringer** **Fins** **Tail**

The leg-rope is attached to your back foot ankle at one end and into the plug on your board, at the other end.

Make sure the swivel is turned out, off to the side of your ankle, otherwise you could get tangled up in the leg-rope cord.

Leg-ropes come in different lengths and thickness for different length boards and different surf conditions.

2 - Choosing a Surfboard for the Beginner

There are special surfboards for beginners. A beginner is best to start on a longer, wider, stable surfboard.

These boards will be less responsive however they are more stable allowing you to catch waves, paddle, stand more easily and not fall off.

Special beginners surfboards have an all over soft padded foam deck and rails with a smooth flat plastic sheen on the bottom.

The fins are small and generally made of soft, flexible plastic.

The overall result is that the beginner will be less likely to hurt themselves or others.

You can also get boards made from other materials, with the same shape that are suitable for beginners.

Once you have mastered the beginner's stage, you will have a greater understanding of what style of surfboard you may prefer to use as an intermediate or advanced surfer.

Soft Fins

The shape of a beginner's board

3 - Transporting and Carrying Your Surfboard

Now let's have a look at how you can transport and carry your surfboard so that it doesn't get damaged.

3.1 Surfboard Covers

Most surfboard damage happens out of the water. Surfers use surfboard covers to protect the surfboard from bumps and knocks and from sun damage.

Travel Cover	***Soft Cover (Sock)***
More substantial form of protection. The travel cover has material with padding. It can be used for daily local use but are specially designed to protect from the hard knocks and bumps that can occur when travelling.	*Thin material cover. For light protection - generally for local use.*

If the fins don't come out of your board, you can wrap your wetsuit or towel up around them to give extra protection.

3.2 Carrying Your Board

3.2.1 Carry Under Your Arm

When carrying your surfboard under your arm, make sure the wax side is away from your body, and the fins are tucked in behind you. This way you do not get wax rubbing against you and your clothing. The fins will also not bump into things or other people. Also hold on to your leg-rope and do not let it drag along the ground behind you. You could trip on it and the velcro will become full of sand.

3.2.2 Car Roof Racks

If you are travelling by car, you can put the surfboard on roof racks.

Place the board with the deck down and fins up. This way, your wax is not being melted directly by the sun. Also, make sure your board is securely fastened to the racks.

3.2.3 Travelling Long Distances

When transporting your surfboard on aircraft, trains or other public transport your surfboard could be damaged when it is being handled. On the whole, surfboards are generally handled well by baggage handlers and top loaded onto other luggage.

However, as surfboards are fragile, it still pays to make sure the board is protected from any knocks or bangs it could receive. Use the appropriate travel covers and you can also use extra padding such as plastic bubble wrap or towels, etc.

3.3 Resting Your Surfboard

When putting your surfboard down on hard surfaces, it is better to place the board down deck first. This protects the bottom and fins. Any damage to these areas can affect the way the board performs in the water.

4 - Waxing Your Surfboard

Wax is applied to the deck of the surfboard to stop you slipping when paddling and standing on your board.

Some beginner boards do not need wax as the deck has a grippy surface texture.

4.1 Applying Wax

Wax should be applied over most of the deck area. That way, wherever you place your feet, you will have grip.

The best way to apply wax is to rub the wax in a circular motion. Before going surfing, check that you have sufficient grip on your board. Apply wax as needed.

4.2 Wax Combs

Once wax is applied to the board, it will gradually become smooth through use. The wax comb is used to scratch up your existing wax cover. This makes the wax rough so you can gain grip. It can also be used for scrapping the wax off your board when it gets too dirty or when you have too much wax making your board heavy.

Wax combs come in the standard size and the key ring size. The key ring size can be attached to your leg-rope or in the pocket of your boardshorts and allows you to comb up your wax whilst out in the surf or on the beach.

After combing your board, rub it down with some wet sand to get rid of any excess wax or balls of wax that have formed.

5 - Cleaning Your Surfboard

When you have finished surfing, wash the salt water and sand off your board. This prevents a salty build up. The leg-rope will also deteriorate faster if the salt is not cleaned off it.

When you have too much wax built up, or the wax has become dirty from dirt and sand, it is time to clean the wax off the board. Too much build up of wax will make your surfboard heavy and less responsive. For maximum performance, have a clean, light coat of wax on your board.

Use your wax comb to scrap off the bulk of the wax. On a hot day, you can use the beach sand to clean off any remaining wax.

Alternatively, you could use special wax remover.

6 - Storing Your Surfboard

Surfboards should be stored in a place where they will not be subjected to knocks and bumps. You can store boards lying down or standing up.

Also ensure that the board is stored out of direct sunlight. Exposure to prolonged sunlight will make your fibreglass surfboard go a brown-yellow colour. Check any manufacturers instructions for how to care for your board.

To stop your leg-rope getting tangled, you can also tie it around your fins when you are carrying or storing the board.

7 - Checking Your Equipment

It is a good idea to ensure your surfboard and equipment is functioning and that nothing has deteriorated or damaged in a way that will affect your surfing. Some things to look out for are:

- Nicks or cuts in your leg-rope
- Fraying string/cord that attaches your leg-rope to your board
- Any serious damage such as large dents that fracture the fibreglass
- Tears or delamination with beginner boards
- Damage to your fins

You should repair the damage or replace the part as necessary.

Frayed string/cord – needs replacing

Chapter 6

Clothing for Surfing

Outcomes...

At the end of this chapter, you will be able to:

- Explain when and why surfers wear boardshorts, rash vests, wetsuits, booties, gloves and surf helmets
- Identify 3 different types of wetsuits
- Explain how wetsuits are constructed

The only piece of clothing that you really need for surfing is bathers/ boardshorts. However, there is a variety of surf clothing available so that you can surf comfortably in all different water and weather conditions.

The main pieces of surf clothing are:
- boardshorts
- wetsuits
- rash vests
- surf helmets
- booties
- gloves

1 - Boardshorts

Boardshorts are the most common piece of surf clothing. The surfer can spend quite a bit of time sitting on the surfboard waiting for waves. As a result, the inside of the thigh rubs against the rails (side) of the surfboard and wax. So, surfers wear boardshorts to protect them from thigh rash.

Boardshorts are a more hardy piece of clothing than lycra/nylon bathers. Lycra/nylon bathers are more likely to tear as they rub against the wax on the surfboard.

2 - Wetsuits

Wetsuits are worn primarily in colder weather and water conditions.

A wetsuit acts like a thermal layer of skin. The material hugs the body keeping your body heat in. It allows a thin layer of water to enter the wetsuit. Your body heat then warms up this water and further helps to keep you warm. Wetsuits are usually made in black material as black is a colour that absorbs the suns rays and heats up quickly.

Wetsuit material is made from flexible rubber and neoprin. This allows the material to fit, and flex, over the body like a glove. As the wetsuit fits tight, it can cause your movements to be slightly restricted.

2.1 Wetsuit Construction

Wetsuits have different thicknesses.

The thicker the wetsuit, the more protection you have from the cold. The thickness of wetsuits ranges from 6mm for very cold water to 2mm for slightly cool conditions.

Thick wetsuits will restrict your movements more than thinner wetsuits.

Due to technological advances, wetsuits are increasingly being made of materials that provide more flexibility and therefore are less restrictive.

Wetsuits also have unsealed or sealed seams.

Unsealed seam wetsuits let water in and out more easily through the stitching meaning the body needs to continually reheat the water in the wetsuit.

Sealed seam wetsuits stop the movement of water entering through the seams allowing you to stay much warmer.

2.2 Types of Wetsuits

Wetsuits come in different types and thicknesses for different water and weather conditions. The most common types of wetsuits are:

Full Suit (Steamer)
This wetsuit usually has long arms and long legs. You can also get a short arm steamer. Steamers are used in cool/cold water conditions. The colder the water, the more thickness you will need in your wetsuit.

Spring Suit
This wetsuit has short legs and short arms (and can sometimes have long arms). Used where weather is slightly cooler. It protects the body from cold water and cool wind yet is less restrictive than a steamer.

Short John
This wetsuit has short legs and no arms. It keeps cool wind off the body and is less restrictive than the spring suit.

2.3 Choosing a Wetsuit

A wetsuit should fit firmly but not too tight. Wetsuits will loosen slightly in the water.

You can buy wetsuits from your surf shop ready made.   Or you can have wetsuits custom-made for you.

An easy way to get a steamer on is to use a plastic bag. Placing the plastic bag over your hands and feet allows the steamer to slide on easily, especially when the wetsuit is damp or wet.

3 - Rash Vests

The next most important piece of clothing is the rash vest. It is like a T-shirt (with short or long arms) and is generally made from lycra.

Rash vests are primarily worn to protect you from getting rash.

They are worn under wetsuits to help prevent rash around the neck and under the arms, where the wetsuit rubs against your skin.

If you are not wearing a wetsuit, rash vests can stop stomach and chest rash from lying on the waxed surfboard.

Rash vests can also be useful in hot climates to stop sunburn and prevent wind chill on cooler days.

4 - Surf Helmets

Surf helmets are made from light plastic with padding inside. Helmets are generally worn to guard against head injuries from your own surfboard or coral reefs.

5 - Booties

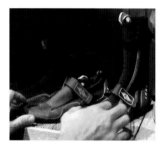

Booties are made from the same material as wetsuits. Booties are usually shaped like a mitten in that there is one space for the big toe and one space for the other toes. Booties are only used in very cold water or for foot protection at dangerous reef breaks.

6 - Gloves

Gloves can be used in very cold water conditions. There are also gloves without finger tips so you can still feel the rail (sides) of the surfboard. Gloves can also be webbed in between the fingers to help gain paddling power. This type of glove can be very useful for people with smaller hands.

Chapter 7

Identify Surfing Locations for the Beginner

Outcomes...

At the end of this chapter, you will be able to:
- Explain the characteristics of the ideal surfing location for the beginner
- Identify whether it is safe to surf at the selected surfing location
- Identify areas in the water where you are not allowed to surf
- Check weather conditions to see if they are suitable for surfing
- Assess food and water requirements

1 - Ideal Beginner Location

As a beginner surfer, the ideal surf location for you to learn to surf is:
- a sandy beach
- areas free from rocks
- areas free from rips
- peeling or crumbling waves
- white water, unless the surf is less than half a metre (1 ½ feet)
- water depth of chest deep or less
- wind less than 20 kilometres (8 miles) per hour
- absence of a shore dump

As a beginner, make sure you surf in these conditions. To surf in different conditions may be dangerous for you and others.

2 - Beach Safety

Before going surfing, check for any surf hazard signs that indicate where it is unsafe to surf. On patrolled beaches, rips and currents are usually identified by signs. In treacherous conditions, beaches can be closed to the public for safety reasons.

Also, look out for signs indicating designated surfboard or swimmers only areas.

3 - Private Property

Most surf spots throughout the world are open to the public. However, sometimes you may want to cross private property to get to a surf break.

Always get permission from landowners or other authorities before crossing private land.

4 - Weather Conditions

Always check weather conditions before you go surfing to make sure conditions are suitable for beginners. You can access surf and weather information from a variety of sources. These include:

• television/radio news reports
• internet weather or surfing web-sites, and even
• newspapers

Weather maps are a good source of information.

When reading weather maps, take note of the high and low pressure systems. Low pressure systems generally produce more wind and so create larger waves, whilst high pressure systems generally produce little wind so there may not be any waves or only small waves.

Telegraph Newspaper, Australia

Also, note how many isobars are present in the low pressure systems. The closer the isobars, the more wind and the more likelihood of large waves.

If there are any cyclones, storms, big swells or strong winds predicted, do not go surfing. Go and watch the more advanced surfers surfing and wait for a day when the conditions are more suitable for beginners.

When you are out surfing always be aware of the weather conditions around you. Weather conditions can change rapidly and before you know it, you might be in a dangerous situation.

Also, it is a good idea to stop surfing about half an hour before the sun starts to go down. It can become dark quickly leaving little time for you to find your way to shore, get dry and change your clothes.

5 - Food and Water

Before going surfing, make sure you have had enough food and water to sustain you.

If you are unsure of the location and think there may not be any water or shops nearby, then it is a good idea to take enough food and water with you.

Chapter 8
Enter and Exit the Water

Outcomes...

At the end of this chapter, you will be able to:
- Understand why surfers do stretching exercises
- Walk the correct way with leg-rope attached to your ankle
- Choose a safe place to enter the water
- Identify how to exit the water safely
- Negotiate small waves

Now we have come to the exciting part of actually getting out into the surf and feeling the thrill of catching one of nature's natural forces – the liquid wave.

This thrilling experience will remain from the first time you are able to paddle out, catch a wave, stand up and ride the wave back into the beach.

You can see the excitement in the faces of new surfers (beginners). You can also hear it in their voices when they explain how they rode a wave back into the beach. This thrill is true for all standards of surfers as every wave is a new experience.

1 - Warm-up

It is a good idea to warm up your muscles with a short run and then do a few stretching exercises before entering the water. Surfing uses most of the muscles in your body and stretching exercises help to reduce the risk of torn muscles and ligaments.

Here are some good stretching exercises:

2 - Entering the Water

Now you are ready to enter the water. Look for a place where there are peeling (spilling) waves of less than half a metre high (1 ½ feet high). Take note of any rip / current signs and stay away from those areas.

Remember to always pull up the slack on your leg-rope when it's attached to your ankle. Otherwise, you will probably end up tripping over it when walking or running to the surf.

When you first enter the water, walk your surfboard out a distance into the surf. This will save a bit of paddling and help you get out past some waves.

Keep the surfboard, by your side, and the nose pointed out to sea.

If the board is positioned across the wave, you could easily get pushed over by the wave pressing against the surface of your board.

Don't be lulled into a false sense of security even if the waves look small. Waves can double up when you least expect it, lift the board and force it back at you. Always be aware.

 Correct

Entering the water safely with surfboard, by your side and pointed out to sea. The main force of the wave easily passes you by.

 *Incorrect*

Board is positioned across the wave. The main force of the wave pushes onto your board and into your body and can cause injury to you.

3 - Negotiating Waves

To get out to the waves you want to catch, you must first get past some of the breaking waves. This can be a bit tricky. However, there are a number of ways you can get out through the waves.

3.1 Carry Your Board over the Wave

You can carry the board over the waves. This is recommended for very small waves and waist deep water only. Remember to keep the board to your side, pointed out to sea. Watch out for any larger waves.

3.2 Holding the Back of the Board

When walking out through small waves, have the board to your side with one hand gripping the tail of the board and the other hand holding the rail closest to you. As the wave approaches, push the tail down so that the nose goes over the wave. Your hand on the rail, keeps the board pointed out to sea.

3.3 Paddling Direct onto the Wave

You can paddle direct onto the wave. This should only be done on very small waves.

Just before the wave hits you, do a push up from your hips allowing the wave to pass easily between your body and the surfboard.

3.4 Diving Under the Wave

You can dive under the wave. This can be used for larger waves. Push the board behind you and dive under. Make sure you check there are no people behind you who could get injured from your board.

Only use this method as a last resort and always check for people behind you.

3.5 Holding the Nose of the Surfboard

You can also hold the nose of the board with your hand and dive under the wave. This method should be used on small waves of less than half a metre (1 ½ feet) only. Always check no-one is behind you, just in case the surfboard breaks free from your grasp.

1 Grab the nose of the board.

2 Whilst holding the nose of your board, push your board under the water's surface.

3 Dive under the wave, continuing to hold onto the nose. Remember to keep a tight grip on the board.

3.6 Eskimo Roll (The Roll-over)

The Eskimo Roll or Roll-over is most commonly used by beginners as a means to get under slightly bigger waves. It is also used by surfers who have longer or thicker boards. As the name suggests, you roll over under the surfboard and allow the wave to pass over you and the board.

1 As the wave is approaching, hold the rails of the board and roll over under the surfboard. At the same time, hold the board down, close to your body but held away from your face.

2 Let the wave pass over you.

3 Then when the wave has passed, roll back up so that you are again on top of the surfboard. Continue to paddle out.

Be careful to time the roll at the right time. You should roll about 1 metre (or 3 feet) from the wave. Do not roll under the impact zone as the full force of the wave will hit you.

3.7 Duck Dive

The duck dive is the most common way for more experienced surfers to get through the surf. The aim of the duck dive is to get you, and the board, beneath the breaking power of the wave and to continue paddling out to where you want to surf from.

The duck dive is also known by other names including the "dolphin through" (Japan).

The duck dive involves using your body weight to push the surfboard under the breaking wave. We will learn more about how to do a duck dive in the Learn to Surf – Intermediate level manual.

4 - Exit the Water

Always be aware of what's happening behind you as you exit the waves.

Shore breaks can suddenly build up and dump with great force.

Be careful here.

Chapter 9

Control of the Surfboard

Outcomes...

At the end of this chapter, you will be able to:

• Understand the importance of paddling
• Paddle correctly
• Lie on the board in the correct position
• Sit on a surfboard
• Turn the surfboard in a sitting position
• Identify ways to get off the surfboard safely
• Explain how to wipe-out safely

Now that you are in the water, you need to be able to manoeuvre yourself and the surfboard. This is best achieved by paddling.

1 - Paddling

Paddling is an essential part of surfing. Many people new to surfing underestimate the importance of being able to paddle well.

Paddling affects your ability to get out to the waves and most importantly, it affects your ability to catch waves.

1.1 How to Paddle

The most effective way to paddle is to stretch one arm in front of the other and pull one arm at a time, back through the water.

As you pull each stroke through, run your arm deeply in the water, keeping your arm next to the rail of the board.   Keep your fingers close together and your hands slightly cupped.

Also, keep your head up and slightly arch your back whilst you are paddling.

1.2   Paddle Effectively

There are 2 main things you need to do to paddle effectively.   These are:

1. Lie on the board in the correct position
2. Keep your legs together

1.2.1 Lie on the Board in the Correct Position

You need to lie on the board in the correct position. This is important as it provides optimum speed without having to use extra effort.

Find the position where the surfboard nose rises only slightly out of the water. This position allows you to paddle easily.

Also position yourself near the centre of the board and along the stringer. If you lie too close to one side of the board, you will fall off or paddling will be difficult.

✔ **Correct position**
The nose is only slightly out of the water.

✗ **Incorrect position: Lying too far forward**
If you are too far forward, the nose of the board will dig into the water creating drag by nose-diving. The faster you paddle, the more the nose of the surfboard will dig into the water and you will probably end up with a mouth full of water!

If you are too far back, the nose will stick up out of the water. This causes strong drag on the tail of the board as it is too deep in the water. It will be difficult for you to paddle.

✘ *Incorrect position: Lying too far back*

If you are too far back, the nose will stick up out of the water. This causes strong drag on the tail of the board as it is too deep in the water. It will be difficult for you to paddle.

1.2.2 Legs Together

The other thing you need to do to paddle effectively is keep your legs together.

Do not dangle your legs over each side of the board as this will create drag.

Learning to paddle with your legs together will force you to find your balance and help the surfboard move freely through the water. It's like riding a bike, the faster you paddle the easier it is to balance.

✘ *Incorrect:* Legs apart   ✔ *Correct:* Legs together

Practice

Practice paddling often and regularly. Paddling is a very tiring exercise! Many of you will have to get your muscles used to it. However, paddling will get easier the more you do it.

2 - Sitting on the Surfboard

When you have paddled out, you should position yourself to wait for waves to catch.

The most common position, when waiting for waves, is to sit on your board. This gives you a better view out to the open ocean where any potential waves will be coming from. If you are lying on your board, small waves can hide your view of incoming swells.

The best way to sit on your surfboard is with your bottom just below the middle half of the board and the surfboard nose a little out of the water.

Let your legs dangle over the sides and use them to help balance against any cross currents or chop in the water.

Your hands can also be placed in the water or on the rails to assist with balance.

2.1 How to Turn the Board Around

Once you identify a wave, you may need to turn your board around so you are in a position to catch the wave.

1 From the paddling position, slide towards the back of the board.

2 Sit up on the board.

3 Hold the rail with one hand. The other hand can be used to paddle and help pivot your body and board on the spot.

4 Kick your legs in opposite directions to spin your body and board around.

3 - Getting off the Surfboard

Just before you start to catch waves, it is important to know how to get off the board and wipe-out safely.

3.1 Rolling Off

The best way to get off the surfboard when lying on the board, is to roll off the side, starting with your legs first.

3.2 Bailing

From a standing position, the most common way to bail is to simply step off the back of the board and fall backwards into the water.

Always be aware of the general depth of the water so you don't hurt yourself when you step off the board.

3.3 Wiping Out

Wiping out or falling off is part of learning to surf. There are many ways of wiping out.

You will naturally practice this many times.

In a wipe-out, try to fall or shallow dive off the board. Don't dive too deep in case the water level is shallow. Remember, try to be aware of how deep the water is where you are surfing.

Be careful when surfacing after a wipeout. Leg-rope recoil can cause your surfboard to spring back at you. Before resurfacing, you can check for tension in your leg-rope. Keep your head down until you feel the tension lessen.

It is also a good idea to come up with your hands first to feel for the location of your surfboard. You don't want to get hit by it.

Chapter 10

Standing on the Surfboard

Outcomes...

At the end of this chapter, you will be able to:

- Determine your leading foot
- Identify if you are goofy or natural foot
- Demonstrate correct stance
- Identify bad stance
- Identify where your feet should be placed on the surfboard
- Explain how to "jump to your feet"
- Identify common mistakes beginners make when standing on the surfboard

Now you are ready to catch and ride some waves.

1 - Positioning Yourself on the Board

First, we need to talk about the correct way to stand and position yourself on the board.

The way you do this will make all the difference to your ability to stay upright and keep on the wave.

There are three main things to do to stand correctly on the surfboard. These are:

1 Determine your leading foot

2 Use the correct stance

3 Feet are correctly placed on the board

1.1 Leading Foot

Surfers ride with one foot in front of the other. The front foot is called the leading foot. It doesn't matter which foot is in front – only which is more comfortable for you.

Once you have decided, you will either be:
- a natural foot, where you stand with your left foot forward, or
- a goofy foot, where you stand with your right foot forward

1.1.1 Natural Foot

If you stand with your left foot forward, you are a "natural foot" surfer.

1.1.2 Goofy Foot

If you stand with your right foot forward, you are a "goofy foot" surfer.

A few surfers can swap their leading foot and this is called "switch foot".

Practice

You can work out whether you are a natural foot or goofy foot prior to entering the water.

Lie on the ground, close your eyes, then jump to your feet with one foot forward. You will find that you naturally put one foot in front of the other.

1.2   Stance

Having the correct stance is important to help you maintain balance and perform manoeuvres. It will also help you to develop "style" which makes for a great surfer.

1.2.1 Correct Stance

The correct stance is achieved when:

- Your legs are apart - approximately shoulder width to help with balance
- Your knees are slightly bent – to help you absorb any bumps on the waves
- Your arms are out slightly from your side with your elbows slightly bent to help you balance
- Your eyes are on the section of wave ahead – to see what is happening to the wave.

✔ Correct Stance:
All surfers here are showing the correct stance.

1.2.2 Bad Stance

Be careful not to fall into bad stance habits when you first start surfing. It will be difficult to control the board and perform manoeuvres.

Here are some bad stance positions:
- **Broad stance.** Legs are too far apart.
- **Narrow stance.** Legs are too close together
- **Legs too straight.**

✗ **Incorrect Stance:** Legs too far apart
Makes turning difficult.

✗ **Incorrect Stance:**
Legs too close together.
Easily unbalanced.

✗ **Incorrect Stance:**
Legs too straight.
No suspension.

Remember:

To maintain your correct stance keep your knees **slightly bent** and **do not have your legs too far apart** or **too close together.**

1.3 Place Feet Correctly on the Board

Now, let's look at where you should position your feet on the board. You should be positioned in the "sweet spot" as this is where your board will perform best.

✔ Correct Stance:

Your feet are placed across the stringer with your feet slightly angled towards to the nose.

Your front foot is placed approximately in the centre of the length of the board - between the nose and tail

Your back foot is positioned roughly over the fins or slightly in front of that point

Any other spot on the board could result in you not being able to stay balanced and/or missing waves. Here's what happens in the water when you are standing too far back or too far forward on the board.

1.3.1 Standing Too Far Back on the Board

Be careful standing up with your feet placed too far back on the surfboard. The nose of the board will lift out of the water and the board will stall and stop. You will miss so many waves by continuing to stand up too far back.

✗ Incorrect

1.3.2 Standing Too Far Forward on the Board

Also be careful standing on the board with your feet placed too far forward. This will result in you nose-diving the surfboard every time.

✗ Incorrect

2 - The Jump Up

Now that you have an idea of the correct standing position, we can talk about how to make the transition from lying on the board to standing. This is sometimes referred to as getting to your feet, the jump up or the pop up.

Here's what you do:

1 Paddle fast for the wave

2 As you lie on the surfboard, hold both rails on either side with your hands positioned under your shoulders, or just slightly behind. Keep your head up looking at the wave ahead.

3 Push up from your knees, maintain your grip on the rails.

4 As you do the push up, spring up off your knees onto your feet, maintaining your grip on the rails to control your balance, at this stage. Keep your head up looking at the wave ahead.

5 Release your hands and COME UP SLOWLY. Keep your knees slightly bent. Your feet should be positioned across the stringer at shoulder width. Your arms are slightly out to your side. Your head is up and looking at the wave ahead. Your back should be fairly straight. The weight of your body should be centered through your feet and onto the board evenly.

Let's see how standing to your feet looks in the water.

1 Paddle fast for the wave

2 As you lie on the surfboard, hold both rails on either side with your hands positioned under your shoulders, or just slightly behind. Keep your head up looking at the wave ahead.

3 Push up from your knees, maintain your grip on the rails.

4 As you do the push up, spring up off your knees onto your feet, maintaining your grip on the rails to control your balance, at this stage. Keep your head up looking at the wave ahead.

5 Release your hands and COME UP SLOWLY. Keep your knees slightly bent. Your feet should be positioned across the stringer at shoulder width. Your arms are slightly out to your side. Your head is up and looking at the wave ahead. Your back should be fairly straight. The weight of your body should be centered through your feet and onto the board evenly.

Practice

You can also practice jumping to your feet when you are not in the water.

This will help tone up your muscles and keep you flexible enough to quickly get your legs up underneath you.

Lie down, chin flat to the ground. Do a push up, from your knees and jump to your feet, then come up slowly. Remember to keep your knees bent. Hold this upper body position, and gently flex up and down from your knees.

For best results, practice this at least 5 to 10 times daily especially before going surfing.

Practice

You can also practice on a bed. As the bed is a little unstable, it has a similar feel to being in the water. You can do this with or without the surfboard.

If you use your surfboard, you will need to remove the fins, as you could cause damage to your bed or the board. Alternatively, make sure your fins are placed off the edge of the bed.

2.1   Common Mistakes in Standing

There are a number of common mistakes that beginners make when trying to stand up.

2.1.1   Standing Without Balance

Standing up without having established your balance at the jump up stage. If you are not balanced at this point, you will probably fall off. Hold onto your rails and come up slowly.

2.1.2   Standing Too Much to One Side

Standing too much to one side of the board. This will result in you falling off that side. You should be trying to stand up in the centre of the board.

2.1.3   Throwing Yourself off the Board

This happens when you have jumped to the crouching position. Then, instead of slowly coming up from that position, you spring up with too much force and actually throw yourself off the board.

Chapter 11

Selecting and Catching Waves

Outcomes...

At the end of this chapter, you will be able to:
- Identify which waves to select
- Apply surf safety when selecting a wave to catch
- Catch a wave
- Identify common mistakes beginners make when selecting waves
- Identify common mistakes beginners make when catching waves

Now that you have your standing position on the board correct and you can jump to your feet with some speed and skill, you are now ready to select and catch a wave.

1 - Select a Wave

Selecting the correct wave to catch is quite a skill.

As a beginner, you will be looking for small peeling waves that are gently breaking. You may even start catching the white water of broken waves.

When you see a wave coming in, decide if you want to catch it. You should first check that no-one else is riding on the wave towards you and that no-one is in your line of surfing. Once you have decided to catch a wave, you should paddle into the right position.

1.1   Common Mistakes in Selecting Waves

Here are some common mistakes beginners make when selecting waves.

1.1.1   Wave Not Going to Break

Selecting a wave that isn't going to break. Only a breaking wave has the energy to push you along.

1.1.2   Closing Out

Selecting a wave that is closing out (dumping). You can easily get dumped by this type of wave.

1.1.3   Not Enough Power

Catching a wave that is too small to carry you along. The wave will not have enough power to allow you to get up on the board. In this case, the wave will pass by you.

2 - Catching a Wave

Once you have selected the wave, you now need to 'catch' it. Here's what you do:

1 While the wave is still 2 to 4 metres (8 to 12 feet) away from you, turn your board towards the shore.

2 Start to paddle. You will need to paddle as fast as you can so that you build up a bit of speed. If you do not build up speed, the wave can push past you.

3 As the wave comes up behind you, you will feel the power of the wave start to push you toward the shore. Once you feel this push, you have the momentum of the wave. In other words, you have caught the wave.

Practice

When you take your first few waves, it is a good idea to remain lying down on the board for the whole length of the wave. This allows you to see how your surfboard responds to the shifting of your weight and turning.

2.1 Common Mistakes in Catching Waves

There are also common mistakes that beginners make when trying to catch waves.

2.1.1 Not Enough Speed

You may not be moving at sufficient speed to catch the wave. As the wave is moving, you also need to be moving close to the wave speed. If you do not have enough speed, the wave will push past you. As a beginner, make sure you start paddling 2 to 4 metres (5 to 12 feet) from the wave.

2.1.2 Standing Up Too Early

Do not attempt to stand up too early – before you have the momentum of the wave. If you stand up any sooner than this, you will be standing up on the back of the wave in flat water, and the wave will continue on to the shore without you.

2.1.3 Standing Up Too Late

Standing up too late, once you have the momentum of the wave.

If you continue to lie on the board, once you have the momentum of the wave, the wave will push you down and out in front. You will move into flat water and slow down. When you finally decide to stand, you will almost have stopped. Then when the wave catches up to you, it will knock you over.

2.1.4 Turning in Front of Wave Too Late

Turning the board around too late in front of the wave. You will not have enough paddling speed to get you onto the wave.

2.1.5 Not Lying on Board in Correct Position

You may not be lying in the correct position on the board. You might be lying too far back or too far forward. This will make paddling difficult and you will not be able to build up enough paddling speed to catch the wave.

Chapter 12
Riding the Wave

> **Outcomes...**
> At the end of this chapter, you will be able to:
> - Angle across the wave
> - Trim along on a wave
> - Identify how to turn on a wave

Now that you have the momentum of the wave and can jump to your feet, you are able to ride along with the wave. When you first start, you will be taking any and every wave you can get and enjoying the thrill of standing up and riding a distance to the shore.

1 - Angle Across Wave

You should now start to learn to angle across the wave so that you can continue to use the momentum of the wave to propel you along.

When you start paddling for the wave, slightly turn the surfboard so that it is on an angle to the approaching wave.

Once you have stood up, you will be able to ride across the wave face.

✔ *Correct*

✖ Incorrect

If you do not angle the surfboard across the wave, you will be heading straight to the shore. You and the surfboard are pushed out in front by the energy of the wave and into flat water. You will find that the surfboard will slow down and then when the wave catches up to you, it will push you off the board.

✖ Incorrect

This surfer is also going straight to the shore and gets pushed off the board by the wave as it catches up.

2 - Trimming

Riding across the wave is called trimming.

It is one of the most basic surfing manoeuvres however it is one of the most important. It forms the basis of being able to perform other surfing manoeuvres.

To trim along the wave, make sure you look straight ahead in one direction. Hold yourself in a balanced position, not moving your body, and allow the surfboard to glide in a straight line across the section of the wave - whether it is a green face or the white water.

3 - Turning

Once you have mastered trimming, you can now turn your board up and down along the wave face.

Turning is a combination of swinging your arms and upper body, leaning as necessary, and shifting your weight to different places in perfect balance over your feet and the board.

To turn the surfboard:

1 Make sure you have the correct stance.

2 Look in the direction you want to turn.

3 Use your arms to move your upper body in the direction of the turn.

4 At the same time, lean your body weight slightly in the direction of the turn. Your board will follow you.

Practice

Practice using your arms and upper body and leaning when riding along the wave. Once you get a feel for this, you will be able to start to make small turns.

Practice

You can also practice turning out of the water.

Riding on a skateboard is excellent practice for learning to turn a surfboard.

It has a very similar feel to a surfboard and the same balance principles.

It takes a combination of skill and balance to turn a surfboard effectively and involves other factors such as body weight transferal relative to the speed you are travelling on the wave.

Your ability to turn the board will help increase the type of manoeuvres you will be able to perform and the length of ride.

These concepts are talked about in more detail in the **Learn to Surf - Intermediate** and **Advanced level** manuals.

Chapter 13

Surfing Etiquette

> **Outcomes...**
> At the end of this chapter, you will be able to:
> • Explain the "dropping in" rule
> • Identify what a surfer should do when they drop in on another surfer
> • Explain what snaking is
> • Explain the give-way rule
> • Apply good surfing ethics

As with all sports, there are rules to follow to ensure the sport remains safe.

1 - Dropping In

In surfing, there is one major rule – the rule of "dropping in". If you do not follow this rule, you will be surfing in a dangerous manner and will get into trouble with more experienced surfers.

Dropping in relates to who has the right of way to surf a particular wave. If more than one surfer catches a wave in the same direction, it can ruin the ride for both surfers. It can also be dangerous as the surfers could collide.

The rule of dropping in states that the surfer who is up and riding inside, closest to the curl, has priority on that wave.

The person who dropped in should immediately get off the wave.

✗ *Incorrect Position* (Drop In)

These surfers are dropping in.

✔ *Correct Position* (Priority)

These surfers are on the inside and have right of way.

This surfer is dropping in and should get off the wave.

This surfer has the right of way on the wave.

It is quite an art for experienced surfers to be on the inside. Not only do you have to choose the best place to catch the wave but you will also be competing with other surfers.

It takes years of skill and experience to judge the right place to catch a wave and could make or break a surfer competing in competitions.

2 - Snaking

Also try to avoid "snaking" other surfers. This is when you paddle to the inside and take the wave from another surfer who is first in the line up to catch the next wave.

Not snaking is about having respect for other surfers.

Share the waves and give everyone a chance to catch them.

Surfer no. 2 is waiting second in the line up.

Surfer no. 2 is now quickly moving to the inside.

Surfer no. 2 is now taking the wave and has snaked surfer no. 1.

3 - Give-way

When you are paddling out, always give way to surfers riding on the wave. They have priority in the water.

Make sure you move towards the broken part of the wave, behind the surfer, so you are not in their way. If you do not have time to move out of the surfers way, then just stay still. Do not panic. Do not throw your surfboard away.

The surfer riding the wave will see you and they will decide if they want to ride above or below you or turn off the wave. If you do not stay still, the surfer riding the wave may end up colliding with you and your surfboard and you will be at fault.

4 - Surfing Ethics

All surfers, no matter what level of skill, should adhere to good surfing ethics.

1. Always be considerate of others in the water
2. Try not to lose your temper
3. Take good advice and directions from more experienced surfers
4. Help others in need
5. Share knowledge

Conclusion

By now you should have a overall understanding of the skills and knowledge required to surf at the beginner level.

Remember practice whenever you can – in or out of the water. Get coaching lessons to help improve your skills. Join your local boardriders club. Watch surf movies and others surfing at the beach. Try to copy what you see the professionals and experienced surfers doing.

If you are having problems in any areas learning to surf, just go back to the related area in this manual and revise and practice until you feel competent.

Happy surfing and share the waves !!

Banks	Sand underneath where the waves break.
Boardshorts	Hardy piece of clothing to wear when surfing.
Booties	Rubber foot cover worn by surfers to protect feet from the cold and/or damage from walking on reef.
Bottom	Underneath part of the surfboard.
Cadet	Very young surfer.
Current	A body of water that usually moves out to sea or across the shore.
Deck	Top of the surfboard where you stand.
Deck pad	Pad on surfboard to provide grip when standing on the board. Also referred to as grip.
Ding	Damage to the surfboard.
Dropping in	Surfing etiquette rule that relates to who has the right to ride on the wave. The surfer who is up and riding closest to the curl (inside) is entitled to the wave.
Duck dive	Manoeuvre to negotiate through a wave. The surfer pushes self and board under the broken wave.
Dumper	Waves that stand up and the top throws over with a great force. Also referred to as a "plunging wave".
Ethics	Good surfing practice where you are considerate of all water users and you share the waves.
Eskimo roll	Manoeuvre to negotiate through a wave. The surfer rolls self and board through the broken wave. Also referred to as a roll over.
Fins	Guiding rudders of the surfboard.
Foam	The broken (white water) part of the wave.
Full suit	Wetsuit that usually has long arms and long legs. Can also get a short arm steamer. Also called a full suit.
Fun board	Surfboard. Same shape as a Malibu with a length under 9 foot. Also called a Fun Board.
Gloves	Rubber hand cover worn by the surfer to protect from the cold and/or to assist in paddling.
Goofy foot	Standing on the surfboard with the right foot forward.
Grip	Pad on surfboard to provide grip when standing on the board. Also referred to as deck pads.
Give way rule	The surfer riding on the wave has priority and you must move out of their way.

Grommet	Very young surfer.
Gun	Short board shape, more tapered towards the nose and tail. Length above 7 to 9 foot or more.
Impact zone	Where all the force of the wave will come down as it throws over.
Leash	Specially designed cord that connects you and the surfboard. The leash is attached to your ankle at one end and at the board, into the plug, at the other end. Also called a leg-rope.
Leg-rope	Specially designed cord that connects you and the surfboard. The leg-rope is attached to your ankle at one end and at the board, into the plug, at the other end. Also called a leash.
Lip	The top or crest of the wave. The part of a wave that rises up then throws out and over.
Long board	A long, wide surfboard with rounded nose. Length usually around 9 foot and over. Also called a Malibu
Malibu	A long, wide surfboard with rounded nose. Length usually around 9 foot and over. Also called a long board
Mini mal	Surfboard same shape as a Malibu with a length under 9 foot. Also called a fun board.
Natural foot	Standing on the surfboard with your left foot forward.
Nose	Front section of the surfboard.
Nose dive	This is where the nose (front) of a surfboard digs into the water's surface and causes the board to stall.
Plunging wave	Wave that stands up and the top throws over with a great force. Also referred to as a "dumper". Not suitable for surfing.
Over the falls	This will happen when you catch a wave and catch it too late, standing up as the lip of the wave throws you over resulting in a wipe out.
Peeling wave	When the top of the wave gently topples down the front of the wave. Suitable for surfing.
Plug	Where leg-rope (leash) is attached to the surfboard.
Rails	The edge (side) of the surfboard between deck and bottom.
Rash vest	T-shirt type of material to help prevent rash and protect from the sun.
Rip	A body of water that usually moves out to sea or across the shore.

Roll-over	Manoeuvre to negotiate through a wave. Often referred to as an Eskimo roll.
Sand bar	Sand underneath shallow water where the waves break.
Short John	Wetsuit that has short legs and no arms.
Short board	Light-weight, thinner surfboard, not as wide as Malibu, more pointed nose, length under 7 foot.
Spring suit	Wetsuit that has short legs and short arms.
Soft cover	Cover for surfboard. Used mostly for local travel. Made from thin material.
Soup	The broken part (white water) part of the wave.
Stringer	The timber strip down the centre of the surfboard providing strength.
Steamer	Wetsuit that usually has long arms and long legs. Can also get a short arm steamer. Also called a full suit.
Surf Helmet	Helmet made from light plastic and worn by the surfer to protect the head.
Swell	Unbroken waves
Sweet spot	The area, when standing on your surfboard, where it will perform at its optimum.
Switch foot	Surfer who has the ability to change their leading foot.
Tail	Back section of the surfboard.
Travel cover	Cover for surfboard. Used for travelling long distances. Made from material and padding.
Trough	The base/bottom of the wave.
Wave curl	The lip of the wave that peels (the breaking part)
Wave face	The concave unbroken part of a wave where most manoeuvres can be performed.
Wax	Special surfboard wax put on surfboard to provide grip when standing on the board.
Wax comb	Special comb used to scratch up your wax cover on your surfboard so you have better grip.
Wetsuit	Piece of clothing that hugs the body to keep you warm.
Wipe out	Falling off when riding a wave.